ADAPTING FOR SURVIVAL

HANDS
AND FEET

WRITTEN BY STEPHEN SAVAGE

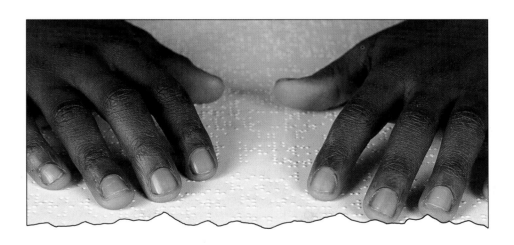

Wayland

ADAPTING FOR SURVIVAL

Titles in the series

• EYES • EARS • NOSES • MOUTHS
• SKIN • HANDS AND FEET

Front cover: A bushbaby held in a human hand and a mallard's feet

Back cover: Human hands and feet

Title page: Sensitive fingertips feeling the tiny raised bumps of Braille writing, which is used by people who are unable to see printed words.

Series editor: Francesca Motisi
Book editor: Jannet King
Designer: Jean Wheeler
Production Controller: Nancy Pitcher

First published in 1995 by
Wayland (Publishers) Ltd
61 Western Road, Hove
East Sussex BN3 1JD, England

British Library Cataloguing in Publication Data
Savage, Stephen
Hands and Feet. - (Adapting for Survival Series)
I. Title II. Series
591.5

ISBN 0-7502-1457-0

Printed and bound in Italy by
L.E.G.O. S.p.A., Vicenza

Typeset by Jean Wheeler

Picture acknowledgements

The publishers would like to thank the following for allowing their photographs to be reproduced in this book. Bruce Coleman Ltd: cover (top/Bob Campbell), (bottom/ May W S P); 4 (top/A J Deane); 6 (bottom/ Mark Boulton); 7 (bottom/Andrew J Purcell); 8 (Rod Williams); 9 (top/Gordon Langsbury); 10 (bottom/Bob & Clara Calhoun); 11 (top/Frank Greenaway); 13 (top/Dr Norman Myers), (bottom/Hermann Brehm); 14 (top/George McCarthy), (bottom/Gerald Cubitt); 15 (Jane Burton); 16 (Jane Burton); 17 (top/John Murray), (bottom/John Shaw); 18 (Jeff Foott); 19 (bottom/Dr Eckart Pott); 20 (top/Gary Retherford), (bottom/Jane Burton); 22 (top/Michael P Price), (bottom/G Ziesler); 23 (Jane Burton); 24 (Hans Reinhard); 25 (top/Jeff Foott Productions); 28 (Peter Davey); 29 (top/A J Deane), (bottom/Jeff Foott Productions). John Cleare Mountain Camera: 5 (bottom). Natural History Photographic Agency (NHPA): 9 (bottom/Andy Rouse); 10 (top/Peter Johnson); 11 (bottom/Dr Ivan Polunin); 12 (Laurie Campbell); 21 (Manfred Danegger); 25 (bottom/Jany Sauvanet). Oxford Scientific Films (OSF): 5 (top/Edward Lee Rue III). Tony Stone Images: 7 (top/James Balog). Stephen Savage: 27 (bottom). Wayland: frontispiece; 5 (top/APM) 27 (top/APM). ZEFA: 19 (top/Res); 26 (M Hoshino).

Contents

Human hands and feet

The hands and feet of humans are adapted to their way of life. Unlike most mammals, humans walk on two legs. We can do this because our feet and toes are able to support the weight of our body. As we do not need our hands for walking, we can use them to reach, grasp, touch and hold things. The human fingers and thumb can be moved independently, allowing us to handle and grip objects effectively.

The human hand is adapted for carrying out tasks that need great precision.

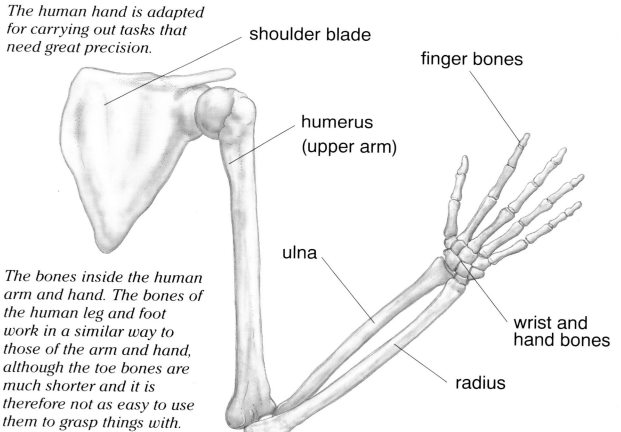

shoulder blade

finger bones

humerus (upper arm)

ulna

wrist and hand bones

radius

The bones inside the human arm and hand. The bones of the human leg and foot work in a similar way to those of the arm and hand, although the toe bones are much shorter and it is therefore not as easy to use them to grasp things with.

4

Our hands are both delicate and strong. We use them constantly in our daily lives, for doing such tasks as tying our shoelaces.

We use our hands to communicate with others. We may wave or shake hands as a greeting, and use our hands to write, draw or produce sign language.

Animals have hands and feet that are adapted to their needs for survival. Some animals walk on four legs, some have many legs, others have wings or fins. Humans are able to improve on nature by wearing special shoes or gloves. Protective gloves allow us to pick up hot objects, spiked shoes help us to run faster and snow shoes stop us sinking in the snow.

This mountain climber is using his hands and arms to cling on to the rock, and his feet and legs to support him.

Four legs

Although most mammals have four legs, these differ greatly in size and shape. Zebra, deer, giraffe and antelope have long legs for running – their main way of escaping danger. A zebra has only one toe on each foot. Antelope and deer have two. These toes are called hooves and they protect the animals' feet as they thunder across the plains.

Camels usually live in deserts so their feet are specially adapted for walking on sand. They have two toes on each foot, joined by a web of skin that stops the camel sinking in soft sand.

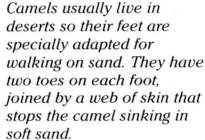

At the first sign of danger a giraffe will run to safety, reaching a speed of 50 kilometres per hour.

Lions, tigers and wolves are hunters. They have short powerful legs for bursts of speed. Lions and tigers have tough pads on the underside of their paws. They have claws that are extended when needed for attack or defence. The cheetah is the fastest land animal, reaching speeds of 96 kilometres per hour over short distances.

Some animals dig with their feet. Rabbits dig burrows to protect themselves against predators. An aardvark uses its powerful clawed feet to dig into termite hills to catch its tiny prey.

▲ *A tiger's back legs are longer and stronger than those at the front, enabling it to leap at its prey.*

▼ *Some four-footed animals have front legs and feet that are bigger than those at the back. This European mole uses the strong claws on its front feet for digging underground tunnels as it searches for worms to eat.*

Grabbing a meal

A monkey uses its fingers to grasp food, just as humans do.

Many mammals use their hands to catch or eat their food. A human may pick fruit by hand and hold it while eating. Apes have hands with similar movements to those of humans and they can easily grasp and handle their food. Monkeys and lemurs will grab a branch and eat the leaves and fruit from it. The nocturnal bushbaby eats fruit and insects. Some can even grab a flying insect out of the air.

Birds of prey have large, clawed feet with which to grab their prey. Some, like the tawny owl, sit motionless on a branch waiting for small creatures to pass by. The peregrine falcon will pluck a bird out of the air with its talons, while a fish eagle can grab a fish from the water with its feet. Some bears and the Indian fishing cat use their paws to scoop a fish from water.

▲ *An osprey uses its sharp talons to grasp the fish it has caught.*

This North American brown bear has caught a salmon with its sharp-clawed paws.

Flight

The wings of an adult wandering albatross measure over 3 metres from wing tip to wing tip. It uses them to glide on currents of air, spending many months at a time over the sea.

Birds are the true masters of the air. Instead of front legs and hands birds have developed wings that allow them to fly, glide or even hover. This ability to fly helps birds to find food, find a mate and avoid danger. Some birds even fly to warmer countries to escape the cold winter weather.

The size and shape of a bird's wings are suited to its needs. Albatross and condor have large wings for soaring and gliding. The hummingbird has small wings which it flaps very fast: 60 times a second. By holding its wings against its body, a peregrine falcon can dive at a speed of 180 kilometres per hour.

Hummingbirds can hover by flapping their wings 60 times in a second as they suck nectar from a flower.

▲ *The delicate leathery wings of a bat are supported by long finger bones.*

▼ *The stretched skin between the limbs of this flying lemur enable it to glide from tree to tree.*

Other animals can fly or glide too! The flying lemur glides by using a skin membrane that connects the arms, legs and tail. Malaysian tree frogs use their heavily webbed feet as parachutes. Humans, whose bodies are not adapted for flight, have to use a machine (such as an aeroplane), or equipment (such as a hang glider), to enable them to fly.

Grooming

Hands and feet are very useful for keeping fur, feathers and hair clean and in good condition. Humans worry a lot about their appearance and spend a great deal of time combing or brushing their hair. An animal's fur or hair protects it against the cold, so it is important that every hair is clean and in the right place.

Cats wash their faces with their front legs and paws, licking them first to make them wet.

Grooming is an important part of a monkey's daily life.

A South African fur seal using its back flippers to reach a troublesome itch.

Mammals that live together in groups (such as apes and monkeys) will often groom each other to remove dirt and irritating bugs. This not only keeps them clean but also helps to strengthen the bond between each member of the group.

Even mammals that spend long periods at sea need to groom. Seals and sea lions do this with their flippers. Seals have front flippers with claws with which they scratch or rub their body. Both seals and sea lions use the clawed toes of the back flippers and can delicately scratch almost any part of their body.

13

Clinging and climbing

Many animals have hands and feet that are good for climbing. The human hand is good for grasping branches and our flexible legs and feet help us to climb. Apes and monkeys are more agile than humans and can leap around in the branches with speed and accuracy. Orang-utans spend most of their lives in tree tops and have a large big toe that helps them to climb. The three-toed sloth is much slower, often hanging from a branch by its hooked claws.

▲ *Many birds have clawed feet that can hold on to a branch. This green woodpecker is grasping the bark with its claws while it searches for insect prey.*

A monkey's hands are adapted for clinging to branches of trees. The big toe is separated from the other toes (as the thumb is from the fingers). In this picture of a baby dusky leaf monkey the big toe on the right foot can be seen all by itself, wrapped around the branch.

The chameleon lizard has special feet that can grip the branch of a tree as effectively as hands. Gecko lizards have special toe pads and can run upside-down on a ceiling or climb a pane of glass!

This tree frog has sticky pads on its toes to help it climb a smooth surface such as a shiny leaf.

Jointed legs

Mammals, including humans, have a skeleton made up of bones that supports and protects their body. Bones do not bend, so the skeleton has joints to allow movement. Try moving your arms and hands about and see how much movement the joints in your shoulders, elbows and wrists give you. Muscles attached to the bones control these movements.

Many small animals, such as insects and crabs, have a hard outer shell that protects them. These animals also have jointed legs that allow them to walk, run, climb, creep or crawl. Insects have six legs, a spider has eight legs and a giant millipede may have over 150 legs. These animals are called arthropods – meaning jointed legs.

An arthropod's jointed outer shell is similar to a suit of armour, giving protection to its owner but allowing movement.

This millipede has dozens of pairs of jointed legs.

Some of these animals have other uses for their legs besides walking. Crickets have ears on their legs; a spider's legs have tiny hairs that help them detect food or danger. Surprisingly, a common shore crab has taste buds on its back pair of legs. A shore crab can also regrow a lost limb.

The grasshopper uses its long powerful back legs to jump away from danger.

Flippers

Even with flippers, these human divers appear awkward and ungainly compared with the dolphins.

Most humans can swim reasonably well by pushing through the water with their hands and by kicking with their feet. Human divers often wear rubber flippers on their feet to reduce the effort needed to push themselves through the water. Flippers are better for swimming than human hands and feet are, so it is not surprising to find that most water sea creatures have flippers or fins.

Flippers help whales and dolphins to glide effortlessly through the water. Seals and sea lions also have flippers. Sea lions swim using their front flippers and can actually walk on land by using all four flippers. When swimming at speed, both seals and sea lions can use their back flippers as brakes.

Marine turtles spend their whole life in the sea, only returning to land to lay their eggs. The turtles struggle up a sandy beach and dig a hole with their flippers. As soon as the eggs are laid, the turtle buries the eggs and returns to the ocean.

Penguins move through the water by using their wings and flippers to propel themselves.

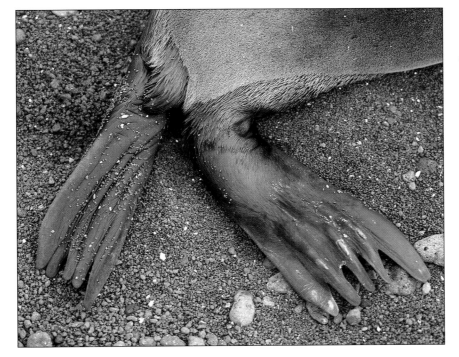

The back flippers of a sea lion, showing the toe bones joined by leathery skin.

Webbed feet and fins

The fins of the lionfish are brightly coloured to warn other animals that they are poisonous.

As fish live in rivers and seas, hands and feet would be of little use to them. Instead, they have delicate fins that vary in size, shape and colour. Fish use these fins for swimming or floating in one place. The pectoral fins on the side of a fish's body help it to change direction.

The fins of some fish have special adaptations. The African mudskipper can use its strong pectoral fins to walk around out of water at low tide. The European gurnard has fins that have become sensitive fingers for finding shellfish and crabs hiding under the sand on the sea-bed.

Mudskippers live mainly in mangrove swamps. These fish can climb tree roots or walk across the mud using their specially adapted pectoral fins.

Ducks, swans and geese have webbed feet that make good paddles when swimming. Their webbed feet also help them to walk on soft mud without sinking. Frogs have webbed feet on their long back legs. At the first sign of danger, a frog will leap to the safety of water.

Swans have to run on the surface of the water to help them take off. They also use their webbed feet as brakes when landing on water.

21

Underwater legs

Not all sea creatures have fins or flippers. Some have legs with which to walk or creep along the sea-bed. The edible crab has eight legs and two large claws for eating shellfish. Starfish have five arms but actually walk using thousands of tube feet.

Common starfish attack and eat mussels by wrapping their arms around a mussel's shell and pulling it open to get at the flesh inside. If a starfish is attacked and loses an arm it can grow a new one. A few types of starfish, including the sea-star, may have as many as twenty arms.

▲ *Jellyfish have no arms, legs or fins. They swim by pulsating their body and catch food with their long stinging-tentacles.*

◀ *A sea-star wrapping itself around a sea urchin.*

Octopus have eight legs with sucking discs on the underside with which to catch crabs, lobsters and occasionally fish. Cuttlefish and squid have ten legs called tentacles. They have eight short tentacles and two longer ones with sucking discs on the end for catching fish and crabs with. The food is captured with the long tentacles and is quickly pulled back to the head and grasped with the other eight.

This octopus is using its flexible legs to pull itself along the sea bottom.

An extra limb

A peacock uses its dazzling tail feathers to attract and impress a female. This large tail does, however, limit a peacock's ability to fly and escape from predators.

Some animals have a tail that can be used for climbing, swimming or for balancing with. Whales, dolphins and fish have a tail adapted for swimming. To swim, a fish moves its tail from side to side, dolphins and whales move their tail up and down. Sea horses swim by using a fin on their back and can rest by holding on to seaweed with their tail.

A bird's tail acts as a rudder, helping it to turn in the air. A fanned out tail and small wing movements help a kestrel to hover in one place as it searches for prey.

A monkey's tail helps it to balance when leaping around in the tree tops. Some kinds of monkey use their tail to hang on to a branch, leaving both hands free for collecting food. Apes, such as gorillas and chimpanzees, do not have a tail. Like us, however, they do have the remains of a tail bone at the base of their spine.

The manatee spends its entire life in water, gently using its large paddle-like tail to move itself along.

Monkeys use their tail as a fifth limb when climbing. The underside of the tip of the tail is naked for better gripping.

Keeping cool or warm

The hands and feet of some animals are adapted to help them control their internal body temperature. A few animals, including humans, sweat a liquid through their limbs and other parts of the body when they are hot. The sweat evaporates from the skin and cools the body down. Many animals, including birds, cannot sweat. Some long-legged birds urinate on their legs. As the liquid dries, it cools the surface of the legs.

Animals that live in cold climates need to retain their body heat. Furry feet help these polar bears to keep warm in icy conditions.

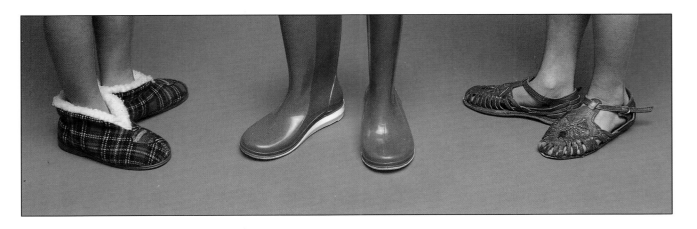

In the desert, the top layer of sand becomes very hot in the heat of the sun. The sand lizard overcomes this problem by walking in shuffling movements that turn over the sand and expose the cooler sand just below the surface.

Sea lions can use the underside of their flippers to help keep them warm or cool. If a sea lion becomes too hot, it can hold a flipper in the air to cool down. It may also press the underside of its flippers in cool, damp sand. This cools the warm blood in the flipper. The cooled blood is then pumped round the rest of the body. A sea lion pup may hold its flippers against its body to keep warm.

Humans wear slippers to keep their feet warm. Wellington boots are a good protection against the rain and sandals are cool in the summer.

After a hot day on the beach, a Californian sea lion takes a dip in the sea and holds up a flipper to help cool off.

Handy things

Human hands are perfectly adapted for making and using tools. We use tools to help us eat, to make things, or for fun. A few animals also use tools. Chimpanzees are well known for this. They use sticks to catch termites and can crack open nuts with a large branch or rock.

A chimpanzee will sometimes use a handful of leaves to soak up water from a shallow stream and then squeeze the water into its mouth. An orang-utan may use a large leaf as an umbrella to shelter underneath when it rains. Sea otters are able to crack the hard shell of a clam by using a rock. Some dwarf mongoose are known to break birds' eggs by smashing them on a rock.

This chimpanzee has prepared a stick to catch insects with. It is carefully pushing the stick into a hole in a rotten tree trunk and will slowly pull it out again. It will then eat the insects hanging from the stick.

Chimpanzees and baboons throw sticks and rocks to defend themselves. Orangutans break off tree branches to throw at predators lurking below them on the forest floor.

Humans use 'tools' every day. A knife and fork help us eat a meal, a nut cracker allows us to get at a tasty nut and we use a hairbrush to make our hair look smart. We also use tools to make machines and build our homes.

▲ This Thai girl is using a knife to make flowers from vegetables.

◀ This sea otter is using a stone to break the hard shell of a clam. The sea otter will search the sea-bed until it finds the best stone for the job.

Glossary

Arthropod A group of animals that have hard bodies and jointed legs, such as crabs, insects and spiders.

Communicate To pass information from one animal (or person) to another.

Glide Travel through the air without flapping wings.

Hover Stay in one place in the air.

Independent Can move on its own.

Limb Leg or arm.

Mangrove A tree that grows near water, sending out lots of twisted roots.

Nocturnal An animal that is active at night.

Pectoral fin A fin on each side of the body, just behind the head, that helps a fish to change direction.

Predator An animal that hunts and kills other animals for food.

Prey An animal that is hunted by another animal for food.

Rudder A movable flat surface at the back of a ship or boat that enables the boat to be moved to the left or right.

Skin membrane A flap of skin.

Talons Sharp, hooked claws.

Books to read

Nature's Secrets Series: *Catching a Meal, Changing Shape, Making a Nest* by Paul Bennett (Wayland Publishers Ltd, 1994)

The Body and How it Works by Steve Parker (Dorling Kindersley, 1987)

Science Facts: *Human Body* by Lionel Bender (Grange Books, 1992)

Further notes

We use our legs and feet for walking upright, leaving our arms and hands free with which to interact with our environment. The bones in the wings of a bird and the flippers of, for example, a dolphin are similar to those of the human arm and hand. The bones of a wing or flipper have become longer, shorter or joined together, depending on the purpose to which they are to be put.

Bones of the human arm and hand

Humerus – The large bone of the upper arm.

Elbow – The joint that allows the lower arm to move independently of the upper arm.

Ulna and Radius – The two long bones in the lower arm. Having two bones allows us to rotate the lower arms and hand.

Wrist bones – Eight wrist bones allow us to move our hands.

Hand bones – Five bones in the hand allow the hands to pick up and grasp objects.

Finger bones – Fingers provide a variety of movements that make our hands so useful.

Cartilage – This is found between bone joints and ensures a smooth action. It also protects the ends of the bones.

Muscles – Various muscles in the arms allow the arms and hands to move in many positions.

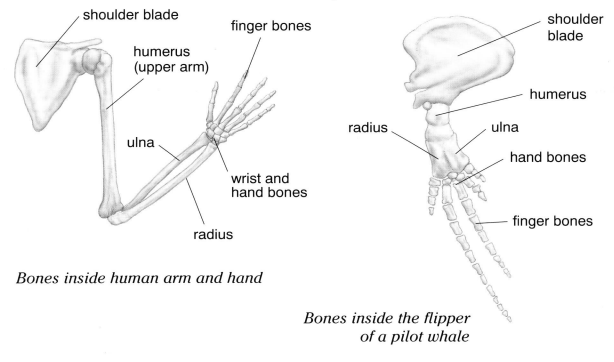

Bones inside human arm and hand

Bones inside the flipper of a pilot whale

Muscles

Muscles in our legs and arms allow the complex movements of both limbs. They work in pairs. Put simply, one muscle in the pair contracts to bend a limb, the other contracts to straighten it again.

Skin and touch

Our entire body is covered in skin. The palms of our hands and soles of our feet are covered in tiny ridges that help us to grip objects. Our whole body is sensitive to touch, but our hands are particularly so and are used to explore the shape and feel of objects. Our sense of touch tells us how strongly to grip an object to pick it up. Each finger and toe is protected by a nail.

Index